James Croxall Palmer

Antarctic Mariner's Song

James Croxall Palmer

Antarctic Mariner's Song

ISBN/EAN: 9783337330538

Printed in Europe, USA, Canada, Australia, Japan

Cover: Foto ©Thomas Meinert / pixelio.de

More available books at **www.hansebooks.com**

Antarctic Mariner's Song:

BY

JAMES CROXALL PALMER, U. S. N.

" Audax nimium qui freta primus
Rate tam fragili perfida rupit."
SENECA.

NEW YORK:

D. VAN NOSTRAND, 192 BROADW:

MDCCCLXVIII.

Antarctic Mariner's Song.

Illustrations,

FROM NATURE.

Preface.

The main facts recounted in the following verses, and particularly in the Notes and Appendix, were gathered from the log-book and other journals of the FLYING-FISH, confirmed by the author's personal experience aboard the PEACOCK, in the U. S. Exploring Expedition of 1838 to 1842.

NEW YORK: 1867.

Antarctic Mariner's Song.

---···

I.

Deep in a far-off, desert bay,[1]
    Begirt by pinnacles of snow,
A lonely bark at anchor lay,
    In Austral twilight's fiery glow.

Too frail a shell, too lightly up-borne
　　On every bubble of the wave,
To face the terrors of Cape Horn,
　　Or stern Antarctic seas to brave.

Far meeter lot once hers, to glide
　　O'er Hudson's bosom bright and still;
Or float becalmed on tranquil tide,
　　Past craggy steep and sloping hill.

Now, like a land-bird blown away
　　By tempests from its happy nest,
She flies before the whirling spray,
　　To seek this dreary place of rest.

Chill night-air through her cordage sings:
　　Her sides the drowsy waters lave;
And, like a gull with folded wings,
　　She sits secure upon the wave;

While, over-head, yon holy sign,

    The southern cross, is in the sky ;

Assurance that an eye divine

    Watches where fleets and swallows fly.

II.

The braying penguin sounds his horn:

   Wild flights of cormorants are screaming

Their croaking welcome to the morn,

   Athwart yon frozen mountains gleaming.

(13)

Fleet as the tern that wakeful springs
  From stunted beech or blighted willow,
Wee, wandering bark, she spreads her wings,
  Once more to essay the treacherous billow.

And such a morning, o'er the face
  Of wintry region, rarely smiled:
For, 'mid the ripples at its base,
  Even the stormy Cape looks mild.[2]

Flushed high with hope, inured to spurn
  Perils by battle, winds or waves,
These eager rovers southward turn,
  To seek new space for human graves.

Ah! had his primal sin that bore
  Man's doom of death, but made him wise,
Not now could luxury or lore
  Tempt us away from Paradise:

From mother fond, gray grandsire old,

   Dear haunts where wedded love had birth,

No thirst for glory, greed of gold,

   Could lure us up and down the earth;

But youth, strength, manhood, wisdom, passed

   In vain pursuit, once doomed to roam,

Fruitless regrets depict at last,

   Bright joys forever left at home.

III.

Fierce winds are up: storm-blasts once more,

    Asserting empire of the main,

Now onward lead with thundering roar,

    Their mingled hosts of hail and rain.

Ice-fiends' congealing breaths uprolled
   In castled clouds piled vast and high,'
Chill back thick-serried billows bold,
   Foaming defiance to the sky.

Deep-down where combs the hollow wave,
   Scared sea-birds swooping find a lee;
But whither thou, while tempests rave?
   What refuge, puny bark, for thee?

Now by the surges upward whirled,
   She totters on their crests of snow;
Anon, precipitately hurled,
   Down topples to the gulf below.

Skies gathering thick their leaden frown,
   Lash her with drifts of cutting sleet:
Mountainous waves boil up, rush down;
   Seas shroud her; foam her winding-sheet.

That dove lone-wandering from the ark,

    To seek her long-deserted nest,

Had vainly hovered round this bark,

    For one dry spot her wing to rest.

Wild, restless creatures of the brine

    With gambols mock her hapless plight:

Loud-snorting herds of fishy swine‘

    Reel, plunge, run races with her flight;

And, in the vortex of her wake,

    High spouts the whale his flood of spray,

Making the waters fairly quake,

    Beneath his flooks' tremendous play.

Serenely sweeps that stately bird,

    Whose wing plumed white with polar snows,

In toilless, ceaseless flight, unstirred,

    Baffles the storm in proud repose;

And, near the roving albatross,

   Pale sheath-bills flicker round and round;

While giddy petrels hop across,

   O'er clefts where janthine might be drowned.`

With oval disk and feeble blaze,

   Slow shrinks away the pallid sun;

And night comes groping through the haze,

   Like guilty ghost in cerements dun.

The dank, raw fog, close-settling down,

   Vaults the drear waste, and hangs its pall

Round the horizon's narrowing zone,

   Where seas heave up their wavy wall.

Outspent, the tempest lulls its howl:

   Winds moan themselves away to sleep;

And darkness broods with sullen scowl,

   Over' the stranger and the deep.

IV.

No sparrow greets the clear, cold morn:

No swain comes forth with carol gay;

But wild the sea-bird's scream is borne;

And thus the sailor chants his lay.

1

Sweetly from the land of roses,

    Sighing comes the northern breeze:

Bland the smile of dawn reposes,

    All in blushes on the seas:

Now within the sleeping sail,

Murmurs soft a gentle gale:

    Ease the sheet off: keep away!

    Glory guides us south to-day.

2

Yonder, see! an icy portal

    Opening lures us to the pole;

And, where never entered mortal,

    Thither speed she to her goal.

Hopes before, and doubts behind,

On we fly before the wind.

    Steady, so! Now, breezes, blow!

    Glory guides, as south we go.

3

Vainly do these gloomy borders
  All their frightful forms oppose:
Vainly frown these frozen warders,
  Mailed in sleet, and helmed in snows:
Though beneath yon ghastly skies,
Curdled all the ocean lies,
  Lash we up its foam anew!
  Dash we all its terrors through!

4

Circled now by columns hoary,
  All this field of fame is ours!
Here to carve a name in story;
  Else a tomb beneath yon towers.
Southward, devious way we trace,
Winding through an icy maze;
  Luff her to—She's through! She's through!
  Glory leads, and we pursue.

Undaunted, though, despite their mirth,
  Still by a certain awe subdued,
They reach the last retreat on earth,
  Where nature hoped for solitude.

Between two icebergs gaunt and pale,
  Gigantic sentinels on post,
Without a welcome or a hail,
  Intrude they on the realm of frost.

In desolation vast and wild,
  Outstretched a mighty ruin lies :
Huge towers on massy ramparts piled :
  High domes whose azure pales the skies.

And surges wash with sullen swash,
  O'er crystal court and sapphire hall,
Through arches rush with furious gush,
  And slowly sap the solid wall.

Cold, cold as death! The sky so bleak,

   Twilight and noon both seem to shiver:

And, starting back from frozen peak,

   The blinking sunbeams quail and quiver.

They smile, those hardy, patient men,

   Though smiles but mock that scene so drear:

They speak; yet words are spent in vain,

   Which only freeze upon the ear;[6]

And when at eve, with downy flake,

   The snow-storm drops its veil around,

Weary may sleep, or watchful wake;

   But both alike in dreams are bound.

V.

Benighted in the fleecy shower,

    Wee wanderer! still she southward creeps;

Now overhung by tottering tower;

    Now all becalmed 'neath jutting steeps.

· Dim through the gloom, pale masses loom,
  Like some vast wintry burial ground :
Here stalking slow in shroud of snow,
  Ghost-like the night-watch tramps his round.

Gray twilight glimmers forth at last :
  The drapery of snow is furled ;
And isles of ice slow-filing past,
  Reveal the confines of the world.

Day marches up yon wide expanse,
  Like herald of eternal dawn ;
But shifting icebergs fast advance,
  And shut him out with shadows wan.

Mountains on hoary mountains high,
  O'ertop the sea-bird's loftiest flight :
All bleak the air ; all bleached the sky ;
  The pent-up, stiffened sea, all white.

Scarce moves she now, mere bank of snow;
    Each sail festooned with gelid frill;
Borne down with drifts her sluggish prow;
    And every rope one icicle.

Amid the fearful stillness round,
    Unbroken by the faintest breezing,
Hist! there—again—that crackling sound—
    That death-watch click—the sea is freezing!

Breathless they listen, trembling not;
    But anxious gaze meets anxious gaze;
And in one flash, one glare of thought,
    Each man lives back his earliest days.

Life-time in that concentered dream!
    Its youth, love, joy; its sin; its pain!
Brief as some meteor's erring gleam;
    And then—that realm of ice again!

Squadrons of icebergs! all arrayed
  Against one frail intruder still;
Ghastly and grim; but terrors fade,
  Before heroic force of will.

Uprise, all life, that gallant crew,
  Prompt action echoing brief command;
Each arm of man now nerved anew,
  With strength from His Almighty hand.

With straining oars and bending spars,
  They dash their icy chains asunder;
Force frozen doors; burst crystal bars;
  And drive the sparkling fragments under.

In fitful gusts, the rising winds
  Wake the still waste with hollow laughter;
While icebergs like beleaguering fiends,
  Close up before and follow after.

Loud whoops the gale; out-swells the sail;
 Quivers her frame to blow on blow;
At every blast one danger past;
 At every bound to meet new foe.

Now to the charge driving amain,
 That fragile bow uprearing high;
Recoiling, rushing on again,
 Making the ice and splinters fly.

Careering, reeling, on her side
 Hove down, with burnished keel all bare,
Righting again with sudden slide;
 Dashing the waters high in air:

Jar—jarring on, each writhing mast,
 Back-stay and shroud now well-nigh riven;
The wild, white canvas strains its fast;
 Frail timbers from their bolts are driven.

On, little bark!   On, yet awhile,
  Across the frozen desert flee!
Yonder behold that welcome smile,
  Sparkling above no ice-bound sea!

Ye baffled monsters! fall behind;
  Nor longer urge pursuit so vain:
One moment more, and rest we find!
  'Tis past—She's safe! She's safe again!

With drooping peak now lying to,
  Where sea-fowl brood she checks her motion,
Like them to plume herself anew,
  In the bright mirror of the ocean.

All signs of strife soon cleared away,
  Northward they turn: God speed them on'
To climes beneath whose genial ray,
  Repose is sweet when toil is done.

VI.

In danger's dread fraternity,

    Friend clings to friend with steadier strain;

And foes in common doom to die,

    By mutual plaint soothe mutual pain:[7]

So these late-snatched from icy grave,

    Friendly before, now brothers grown,

In lives that each had helped to save,

    Regard all others' as their own.

(33)

Thus, while the vessel northward glides,
   Seeking Tahiti's coral shore,
Each to the rest his tale confides,
   Conning their joys and sorrows o'er.

In secret, one had nursed some grief,
   Erewhile too rankling to unfold;
But tears let out brought slow relief,
   And thus his pent-up woes he told:

Monody.[3]

1

The stars may aye their vigils keep,
   Above my boy's unconscious head;
And summer-dews may lightly weep,
   Where tear of mine was never shed:
The winds that idly whistle by,
   May pause to murmur round the stone,
Where never yet a father's sigh,
   Saddened the echoes with its moan.

2

Not once for me the sunny smile

  Beamed like a rainbow through his tear;

Nor knew we mutual love, the while

  He made his short, sad visit here;

And I may die and be forgot,

  Nor e'er the humble right enjoy,

To kneel with her on that far spot,

  Where sleeps our first-born, orphaned boy.

No eye undimmed by pitying tear,

  Save one, perhaps of all most sad:

" Belay now, messmate : try what cheer

  May be aloft there : try it, lad !"

Veni, Parvule.

1

Turn thee, little spirit! turn
  To thy brighter home above:
Linger not below to learn
  All this agony of love:
Heaven yields thee only joy:
Earth has sorrow for thee, boy.

2

Call me not so soon away:
  Never knew I father yet:
While he lingers, let me stay,
  Solace to his Juliet:
Call me not so soon away;
Let me near my mother stay!

3

Seekest thou a father's love?

  Hie thee, gentle spirit, home!

HE awaits thee here above:

  Come then to "OUR FATHER"—come!

Only from thy mother fly,

That her hope may be on high.

She gripes! The main-sheet's trimmed too flat!

  Else, whence this spray on every face?

Sail, ho! Lee bow! Stands North at that!

  Ease off, boys! Here's a live stern-chase!

VII.

Dripping with mist, the rayless day

    Squints through the gloaming, half-awake

The shark swims close to watch for prey,

    And boobies nod on either peak.

Slow drag the hours; with swashing sea,
  And flapping sails, and creaking gear;
Impatience of monotony;
  Longing to greet some friendly ear.

In glimmering halo overhead,
  Halts the dim sun at murky noon;
And fast the shades of evening spread,
  When, hark! they hear a voice, a tune!

The fog no eye, no glass could pierce,
  Vibrates to song, and welcome brings
Familiar strains to eager ears,
  While thus the curtained chorus sings.

An Air from the Icebergs.[9]

1

We gathered a twig from the live-oak tree,

  For a relic of love and of home;

And away we stood for the Polar sea,

With spirits as light, and with hearts as free,

  As the crest of its snow-white foam.

Chorus.

In the happy old Peacock, the lucky old Peacock,

  We jump to the pipe's merry call;

And spread to the gale her saucy tail;

  And dash through the ice and all,

        My boys!

And dash through the ice and all!

2

We got down at last where the sea froze fast,
  And warned us to put her about;
But we thought it a shame for a fowl of her game,
To turn straight back on the course she came;
  So we thumped her right in—and out.

CHORUS.

3

Our pluck did not fail till we lost our tail;
  And then 'twas high time to belay;
But we stuck her clean through; and it came out anew;
And if any man says that this yarn is not true,
  Let him go there himself, some day.[10]

CHORUS.

While yet they sing, a Southern air
  Too light to lift the feathery vane,
Chills down the fog; and, with a cheer,
  They greet their consort on the main.

She too shows battle-scars enow,
  With taffrail crushed and rudder shattered:
Gnawed to the forefoot hangs her bow;
  And channels, bends and quarters battered.

"Lucky," indeed, to 'scape once more,
  From all the dangers she has passed:
"Lucky," to reach her native shore,
  Though broken at the fount at last.

Yet a few days of smiling skies,
  Their common course they both pursue,
Till, scudding North, the strong one flies,
  Leaving her consort lying to.

Flies to her doom : Columbia's surge

   Wails o'er the wreck ignored by fame ;

And only some survivor's dirge,

   Like mine, recalls her honoured name.

Jam Satis Laborum.

1.

My tent beside the Oregon,[1]

   O'erlooks the sullen wave,

Whose turbid waters darkly frown,

   Above the Peacock's grave ;

Where surges weave the shifting sands

   Around her for a pall ;

And, like a spectral sentry, stands

   The toppling overfall.[2]

2.

Mourn not her fate that, round the world,

Thrice circled with the sea,[13]

And thrice to every land unfurled

The banner of the free:

She came to plant her standard fast,

Where it had drooped before;[14]

Content to rest her bones, at last,

Beside it on the shore.

VIII.

Good sailor, when storms are convulsing the deep;
  Sad mortal, whom, haply, misfortune pursues;
Whether dawn break in war-clouds, or stars guard your sleep,
  Live or die, smile or sigh, "*It is all in the cruise.*"

———

  Fair weather makes your sailor sage,
    As fortune fair makes all seem wise;
  And maidens ripening into age,
    Might woo trade-winds and tropic skies.

Bright sun all day; bright stars all night;

   And waves with waves harmonious blending;

Cloud chasing cloud, in fleecy flight;

   Rainbow to shower its radiance lending:

"*All in the cruise!*" Snow-storms forgot,

   The very icebergs' grim array

Lost in the glow of sunnier spot,

   Or melting into myths away.

And now approaching haunts of men,

   The "*sciat alter*" fires each mind:[15]

Some drown, some freeze themselves again:

   Some blow away in gusts of wind.

Sketched on tarpaulin's dingy screen,

   Ice-cliffs in chalk prodigious loom;

And tragically lowers the scene,

   Where the live artist met his doom.

Lovers breathe self-consuming fires,
  To damsels flirting far away;
Or ship-wrecked sons embracing sires,
  For blessings, not remittance, pray.

Each reads, and many spell, aloud
  Their various musings to the rest;
Nor ever more indulgent crowd,
  Hailed the last effort as the best.

Daguerreotypes sun-dried anew,
  In dazzled eyes like mirrors gleam,
Reflecting to complacent view,
  At least one object of esteem.

Back-hair enough for selvagees;
  Ribbons in bows, for marlines handy;
And amulets and recipes;
  And kisses cased in sugar-candy.

But mock them not : however mean,
   However thoughtlessly betrayed,
Each relic brings to mind some scene
   In which the artless actor played.

.

The feather dropped from maiden's crest,
   May weightier prove than vows light-spoken ;
"Ae saxpence brak in twa," may test
   The other half, love's homely token.

And who could scent the withered leaves
   Reluctant fingers half disclose,
Nor wander home with one who weaves
   His descant of a Bridal Rose !

IX.

1

SWEET lady, by whose early care

  My frail and tender bud was nursed;

Embowered amid whose golden hair,

  These petals into fragrance burst;

Dear lady, 'twas my grateful pride

To help to deck thee, beauteous bride!

2

Green as my leaves thy blooming youth:

  Pure as my breath thy holy vow:

Immaculate that virgin truth,

  As the white blossom on thy brow:

Ah! happy heart, thy love, new-born

Amid life's roses, knew no thorn.

3

Limpid the dews from Heaven that wept,

  Adown my stem in summer-air;

Yet sparkled they not while they crept,

  With half the radiance of that tear

Which on thy sunny eyelid shone,

When thou didst cease to be thine own.

4

And when those modest blushes stooped,

To nestle in a lover's breast,

My tiny leaflets also drooped,

And with thy roses were caressed :

So, in a faithful heart, we heard

The echo of his plighted word.

5

A hand as gentle as thine own,

Removed me from that wedded brow:

A voice of low, sweet, plaintive tone,

Pensively, sadly, whispered now,

Fond blessings o'er me for another,

Who loved thee, lady, as thy brother.

6

He, pilgrim on the cheerless deep,

   Where tender flowrets never blow,

Pressed me with kisses to his lip,

   And sighed to see me withered so;

"She knew its early bloom," he said;

"I only know that it is dead."[16]

7

How fondly o'er each faded leaf,

   That lone and loving exile hung!

As if to fancy, or to grief,

   They spoke in some familiar tongue,

Of rural haunt, or garden-shade,

   Where roses lurked and childhood played.

8

But far from home and love away,

  Our weary fate was still to range :

Seas aye the same, day after day ;

  But skies by night in endless change ;

Until the evening-star at last,

Was all our relic of the Past.

9

We wandered where the dreamy palm

  Swayed murmuring o'er the sleeping wave,

And, down through waters clear and calm,

  Peered into depths of coral cave,

Whose echoes never had been stirred

By breath of man or song of bird.''

10

Far beyond fields where gold is sought,

  Onward the roving vessel sped;

Where battles never had been fought,

  Nor blood for glory ever shed;

And where the tame leviathan

Knew not the enmity of man.

11

Domes, towers, palaces of snow,

  Where latent storms lay frozen asleep:

Here silence brooded long ago,

  Over the stern, mysterious deep:

Here, with chilled sense and spirit awed,

Each felt himself alone with God.

12

Beyond the scope of aching sight,

   Lay without limit, save the Pole,

One drifting waste of dismal white,

   Whereon the sun could find no goal;

For, soon as he had touched the plain,

Uprose the jaded orb again.[15]

13

And when day's waning, wearied beam

   Yielded to some long-absent star,

Austral Aurora's glittering gleam[16]

   From sea to zenith flashed; and far

Round the horizon, rainbows rolled,

Inwove with lightning's vivid gold.

14

Ah! how we joyed at length to turn,

  From vales beneath whose shroud of snow,

Callixena and budless fern,

  Pernettia wild, and Juncus grow,

To bathe again in vernal shower,

Or seek repose in lady's bower.

15

But now, where gaudy tulips bloom,

  And lilies fill their cups with dew,

No more my petals breathe perfume,

  Nor blend with fair cheek's varying hue ;

But breath of love more sweet than they;

Smile of my lady far more gay.

16

So, gentle mistress! once again

Intwine me with thy golden hair;

And let those dewy lashes rain

On these dried leaves one single tear;

Then will I envy not their pride

Whose blossoms decked not thee, fair bride.

X.

The sun sets in the ruddy West,

   And "*All the starboard watch*" is set;[?°]

While to their hammocks dive the rest,

   Longing to dream or to forget.

Nor e'er more grateful benison

    Than Boatswain's welcome call bestows ;

Nor music breathing sweeter tone

    Than his, when piping to repose.

What may prove coffin, any day,

    Serves them for cradle, every night ;

And those devoid of grace to pray,

    Might well thank God for cares so light.

No wealth to lose, and none to win ;

    Little to want, and less to get :

"They toil not, neither do they spin ;"

    And waste few thoughts in vain regret.

Let them turn in, then ; let them snore,

    And build air-castles as they may ;

Nor envy them their shadowy shore,

    Their homes in cloud-land, far away.

And if one dreamer fright his mates,

   With visions that may sleep appall,

What soul but so anticipates,

   Sometimes, the final doom of all?

" What ails you, man? What made you hail?"

   But, answer struggling in his throat,

He gasps out, "Are we under sail?

   "Are all aboard? Is she afloat?

" I thought she struck, and, all in bulk,

   "Buried us deep beneath the sands;

"And, some of us, we tried to skulk,

   "When the Archangel piped all hands.

" And then the sea, in one big wave,

   "Rushed out, and left us high and dry;

"And all ashore was grave on grave,

   "Away into the very sky.

"In cold, bare bones, the dusty dead,

  "Bodies and souls and sins unearthed,

"Immortal, doubting whither sped,

  "Crept forth from where they lately berthed.

"And, 'mid the gibbering, palsied throng,

  "One horror-stricken wail I heard,

"From hopeless soul remorseful wrung:

  "I hear it still—Aye, every word!"

The Last Day.

The morning breaks : how long have I been sleeping ?

    Methought I heard a wailing cry,

    Like mourners raise when mortals die :

Methought I saw around my children weeping !

Where be they now ? And wherefore, all alone,

Do I lie here beside this crumbling stone ?

        A hideous glare

        Affrights the air ;

    And, from the hollow firmament,

    Behold the fainting planets rent,

Fly whizzing through the void of space profound ;

    While earthquakes rive the shuddering ground ;

Harsh-clamoring back the summons from the skies,

"ARISE TO JUDGMENT, ALL YE DEAD, ARISE !"

By what strange force, and whither, am I led?

  They call not me! I am not dead!

    Dead! Dead! 'Twas only yesterday,

    I watched my urchins at their play,

    And gloried in their early pride,

    As I beheld them, side by side,

    Striving against their fellows. How!

    Can these be they? These men? The brow

      Of one all gory; and the other—

    Great God! he wields a reeking brand!

    Blood in his eyes! Blood on his hand!

      Stay, murderer, stay! That is thy brother!

Point not to me, accursed fratricide!

I taught thee not—Alas! I taught them pride!

  So for inheritance they strove!

  I taught them pride instead of love:

Thus, by his brother's blow, my twain-born boy! he died.

And she by whom their innocence was nursed,

Ah! where was she, when this volcano burst?

My faithful love! I might have hoped the tomb

Had offered to her heart a peaceful home;

But now, too late, alas! I learn to feel,

In this appalling consciousness of ill,

This awful intuition, that the Soul

Gains not oblivion at life's final goal.

Had I but listened to her pious prayer,

And mocked her not—

        Who passes there?

Phantom-legions all around,

Rise like vapors from the ground:

Earth and sea give up their dead,

All by common impulse led;

All absorbed in common dread.

Swiftly from their coverts glancing,

Each, with furtive look, advancing,

Hides amid the ghastly throng,

Gliding shadowless along.

Though so close together pressing,

Greet they with no word of blessing:

Sound of curse, or sound of prayer,

Wakens not the stagnant air.

Ho! Ho! Ho! 'Tis vain to call—

   'Tis vain: the world is deaf and dumb!

Back my shouts affrighted fall

   Upon my own ear, stunned and numb:

Rumbling as the voice appears,

When we speak with muffled ears:

     Choking as the night-mare's scream,

     Pent up in some horrid dream.

Oh! for the raven's croak, the wolf's fierce howl,

Or boding screech of melancholy owl,

To break this stillness! Music now to hear,

Were any human cry of grief or fear,

To break this awful stillness! Hark! that sound—

Whence? Whence? Diffused so faintly all around,

The balmy dew of some mellifluous strain,

Falls on this sense athirst! Again! Again!

The tender cadence swells and dies away;

And Silence listens for another lay!

*　　*　　*　　*　　*　　*　　*

"I heard no more: one blinding flash

"Burned up the sky: deep darkness fell:

"Ruin rushed down with deafening crash;

"And when I woke, it was in Hell!"

XI.

"Dreams go by contraries," we say;

Death boding wedlock; so they rise

From sleep perturbed, to greet a day

Fit to be dawn in Paradise.

Sweets scent the morn : voluptuous airs
   With sighing kisses woo the sail;
And, glistening through the dew, appears
   The sun, 'mid stars still glancing pale.[21]

O'er coral reefs the surges lave,
   Brimming the turgid, blue lagoon;
And Oumaitia's palm-tops wave,
   Humming their low, unvarying tune.

Tahiti's peaks confront the sky;
   And low Tahara guides her prow,
Till in the shades of Matavai,
   The weary vessel rests.

               And now,

Track her no farther : let her glide,
   For Charon's skiff, on Stygian shore :
Oblivion o'er her rolls its tide,
   As o'er this lay :

          Of neither, more.

Notes,

[1] *Deep in a far-off, desert bay,*   (p. 9.)

ORANGE BAY, TIERRA DEL FUEGO; so called by early Spanish navigators, because they mistook for active volcanoes, a mere phenomenon of refraction, common enough in high latitudes.

[2] *Even the stormy Cape looks mild.*   (p. 14.)

Bright weather welcomed us to sea; and the sternness of Cape Horn relaxed in the sunshine.

[3] *In castled clouds piled vast and high,*   (p. 18.)

Captain Fitzroy, R. N., calls them CUMULONI: they rise before a South-west gale.

[4] *Loud-snorting herds of fishy swine*   (p. 19.)

Porpoises: porcus-piscis

O'er clefts where janthine might be drowned. (p. 20.)

The IANTHINA FRAGILIS is a very delicate nautilus, secreting a purple pigment, from which, it has sometimes been conjectured, the Tyrian dye was derived; but we found that it went immediately into putrefaction, and could not be preserved, even in small quantities. The shell is kept afloat by air-bubbles, so like foam that passing sea-birds often fail to recognize it for their prey.

Which only freeze upon the ear: (p. 25.)

The air near icebergs loses resonance; and the voice sounds muffled.

By mutual plaint soothe mutual pain: (p. 33.)

During the long hours of extreme peril we passed aboard the Peacock, as she shook her strong frame apart under our feet, this natural sentiment, familiar to those accustomed to danger, was strongly demonstrated. Without explanations, or apologies, or any ceremony, persons long cold and estranged, warmed into friendliness; and those who had maintained kindly relations before, grew fraternal. It is almost worth while to be reduced to such a strait, to experience that glow of sensibility, combined even with a certain cheerfulness, lightening the gloom of almost inevitable death.

Monody. (p. 34.)

The incident here related, is neither fictitious nor uncommon. An officer we know of, lost his first child, born two months after its father's departure from home, and dead nearly two years before any letter announced its existence: on a subsequent cruise, the same individual was similarly bereaved of an only daughter, unknown to him, though alive during the first two-thirds of his period of exile; and another officer of this Exploring Expedition, learned, at the Sandwich Islands, then approached only by way of Cape Horn, or the Cape of Good Hope, that all his children were dead.

'An air from the Icebergs. (p. 41.)

Our men's periods of enlistment for the Peacock, expired at Honolulu; and, as sailors were a "happy-go-lucky" set, we tried to buy them back " for a song:" this gave origin to

"The Old Peacock,

A BREEZE

from the unpopular Opera of the

Icebergs."

'"*Let him go there himself, some day.* (p. 42.)

"*Qui mihi non credit, faciat licet ipse periclum.*"

We were backed by the wind and current, against an immense ice-floe, tearing the rudder clean off; and then the ship drifted helplessly against an island containing thirty-two square miles of solid ice, and about a hundred and eighty feet high: this carried away the taffrail and bulwarks, into the starboard gangway; and so the Peacock was despoiled of her " tail."

¹¹ *My tent beside the Oregon,* (p. 44.)

These verses were adapted to two airs in minor, with which the Chinooks invoked ghosts, every night.

¹² *The toppling overfall.* (p. 44.)

Collision of tide and current in Columbia-river, threw up these overfalls into columns apparently twelve feet high: one of these struck a boat from the Peacock, under the bow, and tossed it over, end for end, by the stern, throwing all the crew into the river: they were saved by another boat; and the one capsized was picked up on the coast, about a month afterwards.

¹³ *Thrice circled with the sea,* (p. 45.)

She was wrecked on her third cruise of circumnavigation.

¹⁴ *Where it had drooped before;* (p. 45.)

The possession of Oregon-territory, was then disputed by England; and the right of our flag to fly there, involved a question of war, happily adjusted peacefully.

[15] *The "sciat alter" fires each mind :* (p. 48.)

"Scire tuum nihil est, nisi te scire hoc sciat alter."

Sailors call it "spinning yarns;" but we may translate the old phrase thus :

> For you to know is nothing, so
> Nobody else knows that you know.

[16] *"I only know that it is dead."* (p. 54.)

This may refer to note 8, p. 34.

[17] *Whose echoes never had been stirred*

By breath of man, or song of bird. (p. 55.)

We rowed from the ship, round the base of Tabara, or One-Tree Hill, and found it, at a nearer view, possessed of beauties not promised from our anchorage. The west side was broken into terraces, from which palm-trees overhung the water, with rustling boughs. Our boat floated over a garden of coral, exceeding in luxuriance the richest flower-bed; where buds and blossoms, immature leaflets, and wide-spreading boughs, mingled their infinite variety of colours and of shapes, and fishes more beautiful than butterflies, wantoned from branch to branch.

[18] *Uprose the jaded orb again.* (p. 57.)

January 21, 1840. The sun sets at 10h. 15m. P. M., bearing South, 30° East, magnetic. I often read a pocket-Bible, by broad daylight, at midnight.

[19]*Austral Aurora's glittering gleam*   (p. 57.)

February 7, 1840: U. S. Ship Peacock.

The whole Southern hemisphere was illuminated by the Aurora Australis, exhibited to us only on this occasion, in such wonderful development, and impressing us with a kind of conviction that it never could have occurred so before. Painting, or, if it had been daylight, even daguerreotyping it, would have been impossible, because the panorama was in rapid motion; but there was time enough, as it lasted no less than three minutes. As for describing it, the more exaggerated the terms, the tamer would they prove. A single figure not hyperbolical, may be indulged as a mere apology for incompetency to treat the subject: the halo above us might have emanated from the Divine presence. Yet, that a scene which must always be vividly recalled by those who beheld it, may not be entirely unrepresented to others in more comfortable circumstances at home, though deprived of this glimpse of celestial glory, a mechanical sketch is presented, to be filled up by the imagination; but demonstrative terms must bow to sublimity so far beyond the reach of art.

The Northern hemisphere, though cloudless, and, just a moment before, glittering with stars, becomes suddenly darkened, by contrast; and the southern half of the sky sets the sea ablaze, every wave dashing diamonds in spray. From the zenith, a semicircle of phosphorescence describes itself towards the south; and, down from this, growing more and more brilliant as they diverge in approaching the horizon, streaks of intense prismatic rays, whirl across one another, while the sky seems to whirl in the opposite direction; thus combining red, blue and yellow, into violet, purple, green, and intermediate tints, sometimes producing belts of perfect white; and, between these luminous meridians, zig-zag flashes of lightning play down into the sea; then darkness, as if we were suddenly struck stone-blind: then sharp hail; and finally, calm stars again.

" "_Ill the starboard-watch !"_ (p. 61.)

Night-watches at sea are thus mustered by the Boatswain; and while the starboard-watch is on deck, the port-watch _turns in_, to sleep.

" _The sun 'mid stars still glancing pale._ (p. 72.)

It is not uncommon to see stars in the day-time. Sir John Herschel, at the Cape of Good Hope, showed us the planet Venus, at noon, through his grand telescope; and, at Alexandria in Egypt, we often saw the morning-star close against the sun, at 8 A. M.

Appendix.

.

APPENDIX,

RELATING THE

ANTARCTIC ADVENTURES

OF THE

𝔘𝔫𝔦𝔱𝔢𝔡 𝔖𝔱𝔞𝔱𝔢𝔰' 𝔖𝔠𝔥𝔬𝔬𝔫𝔢𝔯 𝔉𝔩𝔶𝔦𝔫𝔤-𝔉𝔦𝔰𝔥,

IN 1839;

BEING AN EXTRACT FROM THE AUTHOR'S PRIVATE NARRATIVE OF THE
EXPLORING EXPEDITION OF THAT PERIOD.

———————

*   *   *   *   *   *   This little vessel, a New York pilot-boat of 97 tons, was introduced into the squadron, without any addition to the strength of her frame; so that her security among the ice, was to depend altogether on her good qualities as a sea-boat. After some necessary repairs at Orange-Harbour, she put to sea, with a complement of three officers and ten men, under the command of Lieutenant William M. Walker, whose friends took leave of him, with the ominous congratulation that she would, at least, make him "an honourable coffin."

We have already seen that the schooner, finding her boats endangered by the sea, in trying to keep near the Peacock, parted company on the 26th of February. She lay to all that night, and part of the next day, with the sea making a fair breach over her; but, as the gale moderated, she hastened to make sail, and, after a vain attempt to rejoin her consort, proceeded towards their first rendezvous.

APPENDIX.

The weather continued misty, with hard squalls of wind and rain, till the first of March, which was a mild and pleasant day. On the second, they harpooned a cape-porpoise, whose liver supplied a dinner for the men, while its oil replenished their lamp. At midnight, the wind freshened to a gale, so variable in direction that it soon got up a cross sea, in which the little vessel's condition was pitiable. It was impossible to stand on deck without danger of being carried overboard; and below, everything was afloat. Books, and clothes, and cabin-furniture, chased each other from side to side; while bulkheads creaked, and blocks thumped over-head, with a distracting din. This storm lasted without intermission, for thirty-six hours, when the wind and sea abated, and allowed them a little repose; but another hard gale ensued, and then a dead calm, in which they were as much distressed for want of wind, as they had ever been by excess of it.

The next (6th) was a delightful day. Birds swooped around the schooner, and porpoises scampered away from her bow. In the morning, they were diverted from their course, by an appearance of land; and, at midnight, they reached the rendezvous, just in time to encounter a furious tempest. The wind continued, for thirty hours, to blow in heavy squalls; the sea, meanwhile, rolling in mountains over the schooner, and crushing both her boats. A dreadful night succeeded. One of the binnacles was torn from its fastenings, and washed overboard: the helmsman and look-out were severely bruised; and a sea, ripping up the companion-slide, filled the cabin with water. The very creatures of the brine seemed to know the vessel's helplessness; for a large whale came up from the deep, and rubbed his vast sides against her; while the albatross flapped his wing in their faces, and mocked them with his bright black eye.

During a slight intermission, on the ninth of March, they discovered a leak in the bread-room, and shifted some of their stores. It was now decided not to strain the vessel, and waste the season, by beating up to any other rendezvous, but to be governed by the winds: so they stood away for the south, followed by large flocks of terns, albatrosses and petrels, with, here and there, a beautiful sheath-bill, so white that the snow seemed to stain its plumage.

The next day (10th) was spent at the pumps; for the sea toppled over the schooner, and threatened to engulf her. Every seam leaked; every stitch of clothes was wet, and every bed inundated. The men had to swathe their feet in blankets, lest they should freeze; and as the driving sleet fell upon their garments, it congealed there, and incased them with ice. When the gale abated, after a dark and dismal night, they found the foresail split, and the jib, washed from its gaskets, hanging to the stay by a single hank.

They had now made the second rendezvous, in lat. 64° S., long. 90° W.; but, as there was no sign of the Peacock, Mr. Walker thought it his duty to take advantage of a fair wind, and proceed on his course, alone. The condition of the men forbade delays. Five out of a crew of ten, were almost disabled by ulcerated hands and swollen limbs, while the rest suffered from rheumatism and catarrh; yet they continued to perform their duty with fortitude; and no exposure could draw a complaint from them.

APPENDIX.

On a mild and sunny day (13th), the second in that bright succession, the theatre of their ambition opened to view. Two icebergs stood like warders, at the gate of the Antarctic; and, as the little vessel passed between, huge columnar masses, white as the raiment that no fuller bleached, shone like palaces.

> "With opal towers, and battlements adorned
> Of living sapphire."

Soon, however, as if nature, incensed to be tracked by man to her last inclement solitude, had let loose all her furies, the tempest drew a veil of snow over the frozen city, and the vessel became the centre of a little area, walled by piling seas. It is impossible to fancy the awful interest of such a scene, without the pent-up feelings of the spectator, standing where human foot never before intruded, an unwelcome guest in the very den of storms.

They waited some time at the next rendezvous, in hopes of obtaining surgical aid from the Peacock, for three men who were quite disabled. One of these had a fractured rib, to which their nautical ingenuity applied a *woolding* of canvas. and pitch, that did well. This delay lost them a fair wind; but the time was well employed in repairing the boats; after which, though they now despaired of rejoining their consort, Mr. Walker proceeded to the fourth and last place assigned in his orders. The written instructions were thus fulfilled: they had attained the longitude of 150° W.: ice or discovery was to prescribe the bounds of their latitude; and, with feelings in whose enthusiasm past sufferings were forgotten, they turned their faces toward the south. Icebergs soon accumulated fast; and the sea was studded with fragments, detached from the larger islands. The water was much discoloured during the day, and very luminous at night. Penguins appeared in prodigious numbers; and the air swarmed with birds. Whales were numerous beyond the experience of the oldest sailor on board; lashing the sea with their gigantic flooks, and often, in mad career, passing so close to the schooner as to excite apprehension for her safety. A fin-back once kept them company for several hours; and a monstrous right-whale, of greater size than the vessel herself, lay so obstinately in her track, that the men stood by with boat-hooks to bear him off.

Every hour now increased the interest of their situation. A trackless waste lay between them and all human sympathies; and each step removed them farther from society. On the nineteenth of March, they passed between two icebergs 830 feet high, and hove to near one of them, to fill their water-casks. Encompassed by these icy walls, the schooner looked like a skiff, in the moat of some giant's castle; and visions of old romance were recalled, by the blue and purple lights that streamed through the pearly fabrics. The very grandeur of the scene, however, made it joyless. The voice had no resonance: words fell from the lip, and seemed to freeze before they reached the ear; and, as the waves surged with a lazy undulation, the caverns sent back a fitful roar, like moans from some deep dungeon. The atmosphere was always hazy; and the alternation of mist and snow, gave the sky a leaden complexion. When the sun appeared at all, it was only near his meridian height; and they called it "pleasant weather," if stars peeped out but for a moment.

Except when it blew with great violence, ice broke off the sea; but their nights were so pitchy dark, that the deck-officer kept his watch on the fore-castle, and depended upon his ears to warn him of danger. Sometimes, before they dreamed of it, the vessel was overhung by frozen cliffs; and, at twilight one evening, the look-out shouted in a voice of alarm, to shift the helm, when the next moment might have bilged her on a sunken mass. As long as their thermometers lasted, the air remained pretty constant at 32° F., and the water at 29°; and when these useful instruments were broken, they slung some water in a tin pot, and resolved to keep on till it froze. In a stiff breeze, they found it safer to pass to leeward of icebergs; because the larger mass, driving before the wind, drew fragments along in its train; but, in light weather, the contrary was their practice; for then the smaller pieces drifted more rapidly with the sea.

On the twentieth of March, in lat. 69° 05′ 45″ S., long. 96° 21′ 30″ W., many appearances indicated the vicinity of land. The ice became more dense and black; and much of it was streaked with dirt: the water, too, was very turbid, and colder than usual; though they got no bottom with a hundred fathoms of line. When the mist cleared, they found them-selves near a long wall of ice, in piles of irregular height, extending from East by North, to South-west by South, with a pale yellowish blink, indi-cating its presence far beyond. The vessel was now surrounded by thou-sands of little islands, from which it became necessary to extricate her without delay; but, as no visible outlet appeared, it was a difficult matter to thread such a labyrinth. By noon, however, they succeeded in reaching

a more open sea; and the weather cleared up sufficiently to give them
a view of several miles. They coasted along the barrier, till it began to
trend northward; when, night setting in with a dense fog, they hauled by
the wind, and hove her to. In the midwatch, the schooner struck a
floating mass, without, however, sustaining any damage; and, during the
morning of the twenty-first, she ran along several huge stratified islands.
In the afternoon, the sea was clear as far as eye could reach; and their
hopes began to brighten at the thought, that they had passed the French
and Russian limits, and were on the heels of Cook. Every pulse now
beat high with emulation; and, as long as a glimpse of day remained,
they pressed towards the goal under every rag of sail.

Night set in with mist and rain; and, by 9 P. M., it grew so pitchy dark,
that they were reluctantly obliged to heave to, with a fair wind from
the north. At midnight it blew a gale, and they heard a hoarse rumbling
to the southward; but nothing could yet be seen. Soon after, the fog suddenly lifted; and, in the brief interval before it shut down again, a faint
glimmer gave them a startling view. The vessel was beset with ice, whose
pale masses just came in sight through the dim haze, like tombs in some
vast cemetery; and, as the hoar-frost covered the men with its sheet, they
looked like spectres fit for such a haunt. Morning found them in an
amphitheatre of sublime architecture. As the icebergs changed their places
like a shifting scene, the prospect beyond them seemed to reach the Pole.
Day came up this boundless plain. The eye ached for some limit to a
space which the mind could hardly grasp. Mountain against mountain

blended with a sky whose very whiteness was horrible. All things wore the same chilling hue. The vessel looked like a mere snow-bank: every rope was a long icicle: the masts hung down like stalactites from a dome of mist; and the sails flapped as white a wing as the spotless pigeon above them. The stillness was oppressive; but when they spoke, their voices had a hollow sound more painful than silence.

The schooner had become thus involved, by drifting, at an imperceptible rate, within the barrier, while the passage behind her was gradually closed by ice returning from the north. This ice was in large, oblong floes, that floated broadside to the sea, thus lying in contact at their narrowest points, and inclined to revolve around whatever obstacle they encountered at either end. The schooner took advantage of this circumstance, to insinuate herself into every accidental pass; and, when none occurred by the motion of the ice, she had to force her way. This operation was certainly attended with great danger to the hull; and the carpenter assured the commander that the vessel could not endure it; but there was no alternative, except to buffet her through, or be carried to the south; and by 9 A. M. (March 22d) they reached a place of comparative safety, in lat. 70º S., long. 101º W. The remainder of the day was passed amidst innumerable icebergs, of whose proximity they could judge only by the noise of breakers; for it was blowing a stiff gale, and the weather was generally thick. Among the fantastic shapes of these immense structures, dimly seen through the haze, there was one remarkable cavern with a hole above, through which the sea spouted a column of water forty feet high.

APPENDIX.

It was fortunate that the wind lulled towards night; for no object could now be discovered through the impenetrable gloom. A thick coat of ice impeded the motion of the vessel; and it was torture to handle the frozen ropes. Under these circumstances, there was good reason to fear that the rollers might set her against some of the neighbouring islands; but, before midnight, this danger was abated by the lifting of the fog.

(March 23d.) The sun rose clear; but, before long, the mist gathered again, and combined with a heavy fall of snow to obscure the forenoon. Still the day had more bright intervals than usual; and they employed one of these in running to the southward, to examine an illusory appearance of land. At midnight, the southern aurora illuminated the sky with a bright orange glow, dappled with rays of blue, yellow and red, whose sinuous lines flitted across one another, with such a rapid transition that the eye could not define colours so variously blended. This appearance lasted in full brilliancy, for about an hour; and then flickered away in a succession of radiant streaks, followed by a fall of snow.

On the twenty-fourth of March, the schooner was again obliged to force a passage out of the ice, under circumstances truly appalling. The waves began to be stilled by the large snow-flakes that fell unmelted on their surface; and, as the breeze died away into a murmur, a low crepitation, like the clicking of a death-watch, announced that the sea was freezing. Never did fond ear strain for the sigh of love, more anxiously than those devoted men listened to each gasp of the wind, whose breath was now their life. The looks of the crew reproached their commander with having doomed them to a lingering death; and many an eye wandered over the helpless vessel, to estimate how long she might last for fuel. Preparations were hastily made to sheathe the bow, with planks torn up from the cabin-berths; but the congelation was too rapid to permit the sacrifice of time to this precaution. All sail was accordingly crowded on the vessel; and, after a hard struggle of four hours' duration, they had occasion to thank heaven for another signal deliverance.

They had now attained the latitude of 70° 14′ S., and established the impossibility of penetrating further, between 90° and 105° of west longitude. The season was exhausted: the sun already declined towards the north: day dwindled to a few hours; and nothing was to be expected from moon or stars. Under these circumstances, Mr. Walker, after heartily thanking the crew for their zealous co-operation, announced his resolution to return. On the next afternoon, (March 25th), they descried a large sail, and soon after exchanged three cheers with the Peacock. The vessels stood northward together, for several days; when the Flying-Fish was ordered to return to Orange-Harbour, where Lieutenant Walker gave up command, on the eleventh of April ensuing.